FLY GIRL WITH FIBRO
PUSHING THROUGH THE PAIN

xoxo,
Trina Nicole

TRINA NICOLE

Printed in the United States of America
First Printing, Nov 2018
Edited by Dominique Lambright
of DML Editing
Cover Photo by Erica Clayton of
Through her Lens photography

ISBN: 9781730752506

DEDICATION

To my Mom
My biggest supporter
Thank you for showing me
what strength looks like

To the other strong women in my life
My Grandmothers Mary, Phyllis & Sara
My Aunt Linda

To my Boys
Jamier, Isaiah and Elijah
and their dad Blake

With Love.

CONTENTS

ACKNOWLEDGMENTS

Thank you to everyone that has supported me,
believed in me, loved on me, uplifted me,
motivated me or inspired me on this journey.
Thank you for your encouragement and love.

A big thank you to my "ride or die" chicks
Natalie & Abby
for always being there when it counts.

Thank you Ericka, Toya, Nijah, Tia and Larry
for your friendship.

Thank you to my sister Felicia
I know you always got my back.

1 I FEEL GOOD, SOMETIMES I DON'T

Yes, I did just quote Drake in the title. When he rapped that line, *"I feel good, sometimes I don't,"* I felt that. I'm not even being totally honest, it's not sometimes. It is most of the time, damn near all of the time, I don't feel good. It's been a long time since I've truly felt like myself. The vibrant, easy going, likes to have fun, do things spur of the moment type of girl I once was, I am no more. I feel like I've almost been robbed of my identity. I am too young to always be tired, to always be in pain. I feel like a 30-something trapped in the body of an 80-year-old woman. I am just not the girl I used to be.

"Why me?" Maybe the better question is, *"Why not me?"* Who did I think I was to just live my life masquerading as Superwoman? I wore an invisible

cape and an "S" on my chest because I had too. I was the strong one. I held all this shit together. Everybody leaned on me, they came to me for advice, relied on me for support, and I was the shoulder to cry on. I birthed three beautiful boys for God's sake. Who did I think I was? Being strong, resilient, ambitious, and so self-motivated? I was always a go-getter, a "goal-digger", if you may. But, in being those things, I am proof that life will literally stop you in your tracks. It will bitch slap you in the face and tell you to slow the fuck down.

My hands and fingers hurt as I type this. All of my joints are throbbing. But, my determination to get things done won't let me stop tapping the keyboard at 60 words per minute. I stop, take breaks, and keep going. My "new normal" often has me in that routine. Learning to stop and rest when my body says so because if not, it will shut down. And that's no good for anything. I'm not a computer, I can't just "shut down", I got shit to do. Although, sometimes I think people in my life think I am a robot. They think I can do any and everything, all of the time because they were so used to seeing me on auto-pilot for so many years. I guess I can't completely blame them for thinking that.

I think that's the story of many women, particularly women of color. We bear the weight of the world on our shoulders. Eventually though, that weight becomes too heavy and our knees begin to buckle. But, we won't give in. We refuse to be seen as weak. We break our backs; we sacrifice our own well-being for the sake of others. We pretend we are OK when we are not. We hide the pain in our smile, we won't ask for help and if it's offered, we graciously decline. We can do anything and everything, so we think. We endure so much and give so much to others while neglecting ourselves.

One of my favorite quotes, *"you can't pour from an empty cup..."* yet we get so empty that we run on fumes and prayer. I did this. I'm guilty in that, I still do this, even with the conditions I have, I still want to make sure everyone else's needs are taken care of, before my own. I realized that I give and give of myself, even when nothing is left to give. That's like trying to go shopping when your bank account balance is -$100. It's hard to window shop, isn't it? To watch everyone else buy what they want while you look on wishing you had money to spend. That's kind of what it's like having an illness that depletes you, you get to sit on the sidelines feeling miserable while everyone else enjoys life.

I suffer from a few conditions, and unfortunately, none of them can be seen by the naked eye. They are in a class of "invisible illnesses," and it's hard to convince the world around me I don't feel well because I look fine on the outside. I believe when you look good, you feel good, so I try my best to not look like what I go through. And, thank God I don't because I would look a hot damn mess, every day. And ain't nothing cute about that!

Fibromyalgia, Migraines, and Depression are the main culprits robbing me of my time, energy, precious moments with my children, my creativity and, at times, my sanity. Maybe I developed these conditions as a lesson. A painful lesson, but a lesson nonetheless. I need to take better care of myself. My physical, mental, and emotional health is important. *Self-care is important and necessary.* If you, reading this, take nothing else from my words, just remember that.

They are smooth criminals though, these illnesses. *cue Michael Jackson* They come in, uninvited and unsuspecting, whenever they see fit, to trap me in a roller coaster of pain and emotions. It is a never-ending ride of ups and downs. And, to be clear, I hate roller coasters! How is it that these deviants get away with so much and yet, I am the one that feels like a prisoner in my own body? I am trapped in this exhausting cycle.

Now, all I can really do is take it day by day because there are still things to be done. Kids to be cared for, parent-teacher conferences to go to, basketball tournaments to attend, bills to pay, dinner to make, so honestly, all I can do is get up and do it. I still have to be a mom, a sister, a daughter, an auntie, a partner, and a friend. I have many roles and I can't just abandon them because I don't feel good. Sometimes, my life feels like I'm trying to build a sandcastle on quicksand.

A mix of stress, a dash of trauma, sprinkled with a little drama for flavor, sautéed with some poor choices, baked on high for over 30 years, Honey, that is a recipe for disaster!

This is my journey living with these conditions, day to day, and how I am finding my own strength to push through the pain.

2 PAIN PAIN, GO AWAY

I grew up in the 90's the best time, I think, there was to grow up. Hip-hop music and the culture shaped us. I loved Tupac and Biggie (still do). We were fascinated by the East Coast vs West Coast beef. And there's still nothing like 90's R&B. I wanted to be like Aaliyah and in my head I was a part of the girl group TLC. I did the "Tootsie Roll" at school dances. I rocked airbrush t-shirts, baggy jeans and Jodeci boots. If I learned anything from the 90's, it was to always come out of the house "hella fresh".

We were carefree. We rode our bikes all around the city, just as long as we were home before the streetlights came on. Before cell phones, we three-way called our friends and planned to go to the Budget Theater to see $2 movies. I watched *"Martin"*, *"Living Single"*, *"The Fresh Prince of Bel-Air"*, and of course, *"In Living Color"* on TV.

I might not have understood all the jokes but one thing I knew is I loved *"The Fly Girls"*. I wanted to be one. Hell, in my mind I was one! They were really *"All that and a bag of chips"*. They were pretty, they had dope hairstyles, they were stylish and could bust a move! My friends and I would try to imitate their outfits and their dance routines. They may never know how influential they really were but I know they influenced me. I like to think of myself as a modern day "Fly Girl" that just so happens to have Fibromyalgia. I mean, I still rock my bamboo earrings from time to time.

Pain is the name of the game. But, in this game, there is no way to win. I can play the best defense I can and will still feel defeated. Even Phil Jackson's "Triangle Defense" is no match for it (shout out to the 90s Chicago Bulls dream team).

There are bad days and then there are really bad days. Don't get me wrong, there are some good days tossed in there, but those are few and far between. I think I, and others with this condition, are really good at pretending to be OK. We pretend to be

OK on the outside even though our insides feel like we've been beaten with a ton of bricks. And maybe it's more so for other people's comfort. Maybe it's to avoid the never-ending questions and having to explain the condition. Maybe it's to avoid the pity party we didn't ask to be invited too.

You're probably wondering what Fibromyalgia is. Some in the medical community don't even believe it's a real thing. To quote Cher from the movie *"Clueless"*, *"AS IF!"* But, to put it simply, it is widespread pain and tenderness throughout the body. And it sucks. According to mayoclinic.org:

"Fibromyalgia is a disorder characterized by widespread musculoskeletal pain accompanied by fatigue, sleep, memory and mood issues. Researchers believe that Fibromyalgia amplifies painful sensations by affecting the way your brain processes pain signals." Some doctors believe it is an overactive nerve condition.

What sucks even more, is that Fibromyalgia comes with a slew of other symptoms and there is no cure! One can suffer from headaches, brain fog, sleep disturbances, insomnia, fatigue, anxiety, and

9

depression, the list goes on. Every day is different and where the pain is located can differ day by day as well. The intensity of the pain and the way the pain feels varies too. It's so frustrating because you just never know what to expect or how you will feel each day.

It is still unknown what causes it exactly but it seems it can be triggered by stress, trauma, genetics or a combination of all. It is still such a mystery and yet over 3 million people in the US alone suffer from it and it affects women more than men.

I've heard stress has a way of manifesting itself into physical ailments. Perhaps all the stress in my life, the things I don't talk about, the emotions I keep bottled up inside finally revealed themselves as this pain I now endure daily. This enemy that takes over my body, my mind and sometimes, my spirit. Pain that can't be seen by others, so maybe they believe it doesn't exist. I have an "invisible illness" that has altered my entire existence.

Stress and I are low key BFFs. It is always lingering around, some days more present than others. It has become a staple in my life, whether I want it to be there or not. No matter how much I try to limit our time together, it just won't go away. It's like the annoying boyfriend you keep trying to break up with, but he just doesn't get it. *eye roll*

Remember the show, *"Sister, Sister"*? Every day I just want to say to stress, *"Go home, Roger!"* *(Side note: I had the biggest crush on Marques Houston.)* It's that pesky, intrusive, major annoyance that just doesn't seem to take a hint. I believe stress played a major part in me developing this condition and even now it's why my pain won't go away.

Fibromyalgia, for me, feels like a throbbing pain. I get it all over my body, but my lower back, hips and knees hurt the most and the most often. All of my joints are usually affected daily. Other times, it feels like shooting pain in my body.

A "flare-up," can happen at any time and it affects my whole body. It can last a few days to weeks at a time. At times, my body literally feels tender to the touch. Sometimes, I walk with a limp because my hips and knees hurt so badly. Partner that with fatigue and the fact that I can't fall asleep, and if I do I wake up multiple times during the night. That then leads to my energy level being at a 0 or maybe a 3 on a good day. It just feels never-ending. There is no cure for it and the medications approved to treat it, in my opinion, don't work. And I've tried them all.

A flare-up can sneak up on you. When my body is going into flare-up mode, I feel achy all over. Think of how you feel when you're coming down with the flu, it's horrible. I have no energy; I can barely do simple tasks. My body feels like it shuts down on me. All I can do is curl up under a heated blanket and rest as much as I can, if I can.

You ever had an auntie or a grandma that swears when her knees hurt, the rain is coming? Yep. That's me. For some, with Fibromyalgia, even the weather changes can affect how they feel. For me, cold, wet, rainy weather are conditions for an automatic flare-up. Even if I didn't see the weather report, I can usually tell if it will rain because of how my body aches. Moisture and humidity have that effect on me also. It probably isn't helpful that I live in the Midwest, where our winters are long and cold and we have more bad weather than good.

I can't walk for long periods of time. I feel so bad when my kids want to do things like go to Great

America or go to the State Fair. Walking around venues like that is torture for me. By the end of the day, my body is in full flare-up mode. I refuse to get into a wheelchair, so for my kids, I suffer through. Their childhoods shouldn't be cut short because of my pain. I just try to pace myself and sit when I can. I let them know that Mom needs a break and needs to rest.

Brain fog or "Fibro fog", as it's referred too, will have you thinking you are losing your mind! It's a feeling of fuzziness, sometimes forgetfulness that happens. I can be in the middle of doing something and literally stop in my tracks because I forgot what I was doing or what I was saying. People probably think I'm such a ditz when I stop mid-sentence clueless about what I was going to say next. It's easy to get distracted, forget or lose things, and struggle to keep up with conversations. It feels like my brain just turns to Jell-O.

I suffer from migraine headaches so debilitating that I have to seclude myself in a dark, cold room. Imagine your head feeling like it will explode and at the same time you have to make dinner, help with homework and give baths. I have sensitivity to light and sound and they can last from 1 day to a week at a time. Nothing over the counter works for me anymore. I go into the doctor's office and get an injection in my butt that burns like hell but it only takes the edge off. Migraines have also landed me in the ER where the doctors have to give me medication through an IV. They call it a "Migraine Cocktail," and sometimes it's the only thing that works. Yes, they get that bad.

My paternal grandmother, Sara, also suffered from migraines. She tells me all the time, I'm just like her, in the sense that I'm always on the go and I need to slow down. She suffered a brain aneurysm and survived it. She believes it was caused by all the stress in her life. Every time I have a migraine, I'm plagued with fear. *Will this be the time I have an aneurysm? What if I have one and don't survive it? What will happen to my kids?* Thoughts of worry and fear probably make it worse.

When I am feeling sad or defeated in these illnesses, I try not to show it. I don't let onto it and I don't let people know. I keep my sadness at bay. Sometimes, I cry. I cry because the pain is overwhelming. I cry because I feel like nobody understands. I cry because I feel robbed of the woman I used to be. I cry in my pillow when I'm alone, but only after my kids go to sleep because I don't want them to see or hear me. I cry in the shower because the sound of the water drowns out the sound of my sadness. My tears mix in with the water and they disappear down the drain, so nobody ever has to know.

Depression is an underlying symptom of having Fibromyalgia. I don't believe my depression is solely caused by having Fibro, but it got worse as I developed the condition. I mean, how is it not sad to basically be in pain every day? I tried and tried to not go down that road of sorrow and I denied it to my doctor initially. I felt like depression was a black hole I didn't want to get sucked into. I tried to avoid it like the plague, but the thing is you can't control it. And, for me being a slight control-freak, that is hard. Maybe because of the stigma attached to having depression or any kind of mental illness, I didn't want to accept it. I wanted to believe I was strong enough to fight it. With enough willpower, I can tackle anything life throws at me. At one point, I wanted to be an actress, so it's easy for me to play the role of being happy.

My therapist classified it as *"High-Functioning Depression"*. Basically, I'm sad on the inside, but I still get up and do what I got to do. I don't "look" depressed, but inwardly, I'm dealing with a lot of bullshit. Not sure if depression really has a look, but since I'm not curled up in my bed, in the dark, secluded from the world, maybe people don't believe my depression is real. My energy is depleted most of the time, small tasks feel like huge tasks. I worry a lot. I have the innate inability to rest or slow down. I strive for perfection. I've always been a perfectionist, from my grades, to my jobs, just in life. I always want to be the best in what I do and I. Hate. To. Fail. It's unacceptable. I put these unrealistic expectations on myself and when I don't achieve them, I get upset. I've always been this way.

I can remember in the third grade, we had to do a project and presentation on a dinosaur. I took it upon myself to make a big ass 2-foot model of a Triceratops made of paper mache and brown paint. I made his horns out of toilet paper tubes. I cut green paper leaves coming out of his mouth to show he was an herbivore. It took me the whole weekend to complete and honestly, it was the best in the class. I didn't think about how hard it would be to carry it on the bus though! But even at 8 years old, I wanted to get the best grade and have the best project. That perfectionism followed me throughout school. And, it's no wonder, I carried that into adulthood.

It took me now being in my 30s to realize, I don't have to be perfect. *It's actually OK to not be OK.* Through enough trials and tribulations, I've come to those realizations. I'm not perfect, despite what my Instagram posts may show. Nobody is expecting me to be perfect, I don't have to pretend that I'm perfect and there is no such thing as perfection. I don't have to sit on this self-made pedestal and strive for these goals, on these unrealistic timelines, that I set for myself. Life has a way of messing up all of your plans anyway, so you might as well go with the flow. I'm learning. And listen, small progress is still progress. Am I completely perfection-striving free? No. But I'm getting there and that alone reduces some of the self-inflicted stress in my life.

The newest condition to hit me is Vertigo. I don't know if it is directly related to Fibromyalgia or not, but it can be associated with migraine headaches, which I get frequently. According to WebMD, *"Vertigo is a sensation of feeling off balance. If you have these dizzy spells, you might feel like you are spinning or that the world around you is spinning."* It is thought to be caused by an inner ear problem. I didn't know what was happening. The first time I experienced it, I was dizzy and felt very off balance. I went for a few days in a dazed-like state. I also had a persistent headache and nausea. I probably couldn't walk a straight line if I were asked to. After going to the Urgent care and it being diagnosed as "Vertigo", I was prescribed a motion sickness medication and told to do some movements with my head. It lasted a week and now it's just another condition to add to my list of ailments.

3 CHILDHOOD BE LIKE

C hildhood is innocence. It should be full of joy, happy moments and gleeful memories you always carry with you. Mostly, my childhood was good. My mom did the best she could to take care of us. She struggled to pay the bills, but we never went without. We always had a roof over our head, food in our bellies and clothes on our backs. My hair bows, matched my earrings, which matched my socks. We were always neat and clean. The way my mom presented us to the world, you would never know how hard she struggled.

But, things that happen in our childhood we often carry into adulthood. Sometimes we carry those things unintentionally and maybe even subconsciously. Our childhood and adolescence help mold us into the adults we will be, but sometimes those childhood memories can haunt us.

One of the most daunting, scary, and traumatic events happened when I was maybe six or seven. I often spent my summers back in Indiana with my mom's side of the family. My great-grandma's house is where the cousins would gather and have fun together. We would go out of her back door, cross the alley to get to the "Dairy Queen", to get yummy Dilly bars or slushies on hot summer days. We would walk across Broadway Street to the Shell gas station for snacks.

One day, my cousin, her friend, and I crossed the busy street and were walking towards the gas station. A woman and a man were sitting in their car at the pump. The lady got out of the passenger side of a pale yellow, long boat like car, not quite sure but maybe it was a Cadillac. She was calling for me to come to her. She kept motioning her hands for me to come in her direction. I profusely shook my head no. I was terrified. She came closer and closer until my cousin and friend grabbed me. They sandwiched me in between them. The gas station attendant saw what was happening and ran out to help. We hurried into the gas station and she pushed us behind the counter.

The attendant called my great-grandma Minnie to come get us. I remember peering through the dirty gas station window watching her stand on the corner with her snow-white hair waiting to cross the busy street to come to our rescue. Thinking back, I don't really know what a 70-something great-grandma could have done, but in that moment, she was my superhero coming to save the day. I remember nothing that was said in the commotion, but I vividly remember the events of that day. It makes me now hyper-aware of my surroundings and a little paranoid because I am alone more often than not. It's probably why I don't let my own kids too far out of my sight since I was almost kidnapped. I don't remember us ever walking back to that gas station for snacks again.

My first experience with racism was in Kindergarten. My mom enrolled me in Chapter 220, which was the inter-district integration transfer program. Basically, little black and brown kids could go to school out in the suburbs. I knew going into K-5 I was different from the other kids. There was nobody else that looked like me. I remember playing by myself most of the time. One day this little boy told me, *"We don't like brown kids here."* And that was my introduction to how cruel kids could be.

My mom transferred me into another Chapter 220 school that was a little better, but the overall ratio of black to white kids was still very low. There were more of them than us. There was a group of maybe 10 of us in my grade, and we tried to stick together as much as we could. When you are in white spaces you are very aware of your blackness, even in elementary school. We were always aware of what we did, what we said, and what we wore because we didn't want to bring any attention to ourselves. We tried to not be troublemakers and just do as we were told. We really didn't know any better.

I was always trying to outdo and outperform the white kids. I wanted to prove that I was just as good, if not better than them, despite my upbringing or circumstances. We were kids from the "hood" going to school in an upper-class Jewish community. Their parents were doctors and lawyers, they drove BMWs and Mercedes Benz, and we went to sleepovers in mini-mansions. Meanwhile, we lived in subsidized housing, rode the City bus, and ate food bought with food stamps. It was two totally different worlds.

I remember being in the 5th grade, playing at recess. We were having fun on the monkey bars and jungle gym. Apparently, we were taking too long, and this white boy wanted a turn. He screamed at us, *"Hurry up you Niggers!"* It was like we instantly time traveled back to the 1950s. We were shocked. What was even more shocking was that the teachers didn't seem to care he said it. He didn't even get into trouble. Everybody just went about their day as if nothing had happened. At 10 years old, I knew it wasn't right but felt helpless in what I could do about it.

I got glasses in the 4th grade and not the cute ones, the ones that Medicaid paid for. The thick, coke bottle, dorky ass glasses and I hated them. Then, in the 7th grade, I got braces. I was such a nerd. I had glasses, braces, and I played the cello in Orchestra. I always had my nose in a book and would ask my teachers for extra credit homework. Middle school would be the beginning of my first experiences with bullying. The tight-knit crew I once had, some of them eventually turned on me. They made fun of me, taunting me on the school bus, and stopped inviting me to parties. My ears stuck out so they called me *"Dumbo"* and *"Minnie Mouse"*. A bad case of eczema above my upper lip got me the nickname, *"Bubble Lips"*. I couldn't believe my once friends were now my enemies.

By 8th grade, I got contact lenses, my boobs finally made an appearance and my hips were curvy. I learned how to flat iron my untamed curls straight and dressed more girly. I was a tomboy until that point. I finally felt pretty. I was over the school and the kids and I begged my mom to let me go to an inner city high school and she agreed. I was over being out in the "burbs". I wanted to be with my own people. But, I should've just stayed my ass put! Going to a predominantly black high school as a half-Latina, half-black girl, I didn't realize I would have such a hard time.

I met my first boyfriend the summer going into freshman year. I discovered that we would be going to the same high school and I was excited! He was a grade ahead of me. New school, new environment, new friends, and a new boyfriend! It seemed like the stars finally aligned for me and high school would be great! I had left the suburbs behind along with those fake friends. Turns out, the joke was on me.

I hated high school! To this day, I say it was one of the worst times of my life. I didn't know that my new boyfriend was a popular, football playing, lady's man. As soon as word got around that I was his girlfriend, the upper-class girls were on my heels. Damn near every day, some girl was coming up to me about him. They wanted to argue and fight, something I was not used to in my old school.

Girls would come up to me and say, *"You think you're all that, don't you?"* I would hear about girls talking about me behind my back and how they were going to "jump" me after school. I had long hair and they threatened to cut off my ponytail. I was at a new school, so I didn't have many friends. It was miserable, but I never let them see me sweat.

One day, my boyfriend skipped school with his friend and two other freshman girls. They had sex with the girls and then took pictures of them naked. He then printed the pictures and passed them around the school. Because people knew that was my boyfriend, word got around school it was me in the pictures! I was devastated. Even teachers were coming up to me saying *"What were you thinking?!"*

I had to plead to everyone that it wasn't me! But it seemed nobody believed me. My name was being dragged through the mud and I didn't even do anything! The word around school was that I was a "hoe" and rumors circulated that I was having sex with different guys. One boy even told people he had me at the hotel licking whip cream and strawberries off of my body! Maybe people believed the rumors because I was a curvy 15-year-old with ass and titties. I was "thick" and a senior boy gave me the name "Big Booty Trina", even though my butt wasn't really that big. I walked around with the invisible *"A"* on my chest like the book, *"The Scarlet Letter",* which we just so happened to have read in English class. I felt like the modern-day Hester Prynne.

My boyfriend not only hurt me but humiliated me. Imagine, not only being cheated on but everybody knew about it. He was my first love. We talked on the phone every night until we fell asleep. He was my first kiss and the first boy to tell me he loved me. I was only 15, I now know it was only puppy love, but back then I thought it was real love. I just couldn't understand why he would hurt me so much if he loved me. I struggled with feelings of insecurity, low self-esteem, and low self-worth. I don't think he ever apologized for the hurt he caused. I didn't think love could bring so much heartache.

Looking back, I'm sure I had undiagnosed depression. I didn't know how to express what I was feeling or even who to tell. I was so sad and I hated my life. I started drinking alcohol and smoking weed. I thought it was fun and cool but I was really just trying to numb my inner pain and turmoil. I liked to party. Whatever house party was going on, I was there. I partied all night and slept all day. I skipped school and basically dropped out the second half of my sophomore year. I eventually just stopped going altogether because I hated it so much.

To make matters worse, my mom and I didn't get along. We were always fighting and at a time when

I really felt like I needed her, she wasn't there. And, I get it now, she worked a lot and was trying to live her own life, but back then I didn't see it like that. I just felt like a lost little girl trying to make her way through the world alone.

I forged my mom's signature and transferred myself out of that high school and enrolled into a smaller, charter school. I thought I would have an easier time in a new, smaller environment. But, smaller doesn't always mean better. Being in a school with fewer kids only made rumors, gossip, and drama spread faster than wildfire. There was another set of girls dead set on not liking me and they didn't even know me. And that would be the story of my life, even into adulthood. People making assumptions about me without ever getting to know me. I guess because I'm a mixed, light-skinned girl with "good" hair (whatever that means), I think I'm better than everybody, which was and still is, the furthest thing from the truth. I know my shit stinks just like everyone else's.

That smaller school would be my first experience with being suspended from school. This one girl was set on making my life hell every day. To this day I still don't know what her problem with me was. She would harass me in the hallways and convinced other girls not to like me too.

One day in Math class, shit finally hit the fan. I tried so hard not to feed into the bs, but she was behind me talking so much shit I finally got up and snapped. We were arguing back and forth almost about to fight until the teacher stepped in. I got a suspension behind that and mysteriously my car window had been busted out right in front of the school. I would have a few more episodes like that with other girls in that school. I just couldn't catch a break.

They always say good girls love bad boys and I was no exception. I met my kids' father when I was 16 and he was everything I should've ran away from. Maybe it was his swag that made me gravitate towards him when I should've been pulling away. He was from the streets, but he made me feel special. Maybe it was game he was running on me, or me just needing to feel something, because by that time I just felt empty. I fell for him. When I met him he was on house arrest and had a child. I knew everything about him was wrong but that didn't keep it from feeling right.

He would pick me up from school in his pimped out big body Buick with red candy paint, rims, and TVs in the headrests. He gave me money whenever I asked, got my hair and nails done and took me shopping. The feeling of being taken care of overrode any feelings of doubt I had about him. I knew he was no good for me but sometimes love is blind, and we don't always see what's right in front of us.

About a year later, I was 17 and pregnant. I went to Planned Parenthood, put myself on birth control and still got pregnant! I still had high hopes, dreams, and aspirations for myself but now it felt like my life was ruined.

I missed so much school because I was so sick with the pregnancy. I worked my ass off to complete my regular coursework and additional classes through the local community college so I could graduate on time. I was the "Pregnant Prom Queen" at the Senior Prom. I waddled across the stage at my high school graduation 7 months pregnant. I still managed to be voted "Student of the Year" at graduation and received a small scholarship for college. It was proof that despite your circumstances, you can still manage to achieve things when you work hard.

I graduated in May and I had my first son in July when I was 18 years old. Just like my own mom, I was a baby having a baby. My dream to attend Clark Atlanta University to study Mass Communications was shattered. Yes, I knew abortion was an option, but it wasn't the best option for me. And I couldn't fathom giving my baby up for adoption. I already knew how much harder my life would be by having a baby so young. I watched my mom struggle to make ends meet and I knew early on that's not the life I wanted for myself, and yet here I was.

4 BABY MAMA BLUES

My first pregnancy was rough and although I had my mom and his dad was around, I still felt like I was in it all alone. The myth that morning sickness is just in the morning, that's a lie. I was sick all day, every day for the entire pregnancy. I went into labor after being a week overdue. I checked into the hospital at 2am and labored for 17 hours with no progress. My contractions were strong, but I wasn't dilating. I waddled through the hallways of the hospital with my Aunt. She convinced me to take low, deep breaths and "moo like a cow" through every contraction. I'm sure everyone was looking at me crazy as I mooed my way through labor, but it helped with getting through each painful contraction. I wanted no pain medication. I felt like birthing was what my body was designed to do, so I wanted to do it naturally.

All of my ideas of having a natural birth and my carefully thought out birth plan went out the window when I was rushed into an emergency C-section. My baby's umbilical cord got wrapped around his neck. His heart rate plummeted with every contraction as the umbilical cord tightened cutting off his oxygen supply. They were scared he would suffocate.

They rushed me into the operating room. Everything seemed to move at 100 mph. The overhead lights were blinding. The room was cold and sterile. The anesthesiologist administered a spinal tap and as I lay there, waiting to be operated on, I was sobbing. Fear of the unknown paralyzed me more than anesthesia ever could. What if my baby didn't make it? This was my first time ever being in a hospital and having surgery and I wasn't sure my baby would survive. It was terrifying as a young mother.

Fear took over my body as I trembled on the table. I couldn't control it as tears poured from my eyes. I looked over at his dad, dressed in blue hospital scrubs, wondering why he wasn't crying or why he didn't seem as scared as me. He was stone-faced.

Maybe he was trying to be the strong one. I didn't have time to wonder, because before I knew it, he was born. I waited anxiously to hear his cry. His cry, as he took his first breaths of life, was like music to my ears. He was healthy and he was perfect at 6 lbs. 7 oz. and 18 inches long.

My joy was short lived. Hours after delivery, I developed a uterine infection. I was so sick that my plans to breastfeed were snatched away. I barely had the energy to hold my baby or let alone try to feed him. I couldn't breastfeed because my milk was tainted with high doses of antibiotics to get the infection under control. The illness was running rampant in my body. I had a 104 fever, chills, aches, and pain all over. I could barely walk and there was constant concern about me developing blood clots in my legs. One minute I was burning hot, the next minute I was freezing cold. That infection kept me in the hospital for almost two weeks and even when they discharged me, it still wasn't completely cleared up.

I was trying to fight off an infection, heal from a major surgery and care for a newborn. This was my first experience with complete exhaustion. I was physically, mentally and emotionally drained. My mom was in nursing school and his dad, well, he was a 19-year-old out doing what 19-year-old boys do. I was often left alone to fend for myself and my baby because I didn't have a choice, he depended on me. I suffered from the "baby blues" and was harboring some resentment towards his dad because he wasn't as supportive as I needed him to be. I felt abandoned by everybody that claimed they loved me. I realized I had to tap into the inner strength deep down inside if I was going to get through it all.

Six months later, that same infection landed me back into the ER. It had never completely cleared up. It just festered, waiting to bring me back down. After a few days in the ER, they finally got the infection to subside and I was released.

As if all of this wasn't enough, shortly after, I found out that my son's father had another baby! He never even told me another girl was pregnant! This was the beginning of our decline. Our son and his daughter are only 4 months apart and he already had another daughter. So, I was now 1 of 3 baby mamas! I literally was everything I never wanted to be. I felt like I was just another statistic. A teenage, struggling, single mother dealing with all kinds of baby mama drama. This was no life for an 18-year-old. I was in a dysfunctional relationship but the mirage of love made me keep dealing with him. I'm guilty, in that, I give people way too many chances often at the expense of my own well-being.

This was not the life I imagined for myself. I was completely devastated. I felt the ultimate betrayal by a man that said he loved me. It ate away at my trust, my confidence, and my self-esteem. I couldn't figure out what I had done to make him cheat. Did I not love him enough? Was I not pretty to him anymore? Did he even love me? Did either of us even know what love was? How could he look me in my face and lie?

It took me years to realize that his actions had nothing to do with me. Those were his decisions and choices to make and no amount of me loving him would change that. He had to change and be better because he wanted too. You can't keep a man that doesn't want to be kept. Especially when he is young.

I was emotionally bruised. I had been through so much in such a short amount of time, yet it was only the beginning.

In 2008, I was t-boned in a car accident. The uninsured driver slammed into me on the driver's side and sent my car up the curb and onto the sidewalk. It was like slow motion, yet it happened so fast. My new car sat on the sidewalk billowing smoke and it was totaled. The windshield shattered. I suffered from whiplash and my head smacked into the driver's side door. I was lucky because the accident could have been way worse. I sustained only minor injuries, but my body was flooded with pain. A pinched nerve in my neck kept me in physical therapy and contributed to persistent, ongoing headaches. My neck and shoulders were so stiff; I could barely turn my head in any direction. It took a long time before I could get the sound of crashing metal and shattering glass out of my head.

My son's father and I had been off and on, off and on. Five and a half years later, I found myself pregnant again and that pregnancy was worse than the one before. The morning sickness never went away, again. I was often dizzy, suffered from bad headaches, terrible back pain and I was passing out. They could never pinpoint the cause of me passing out, so I was put on bedrest. I couldn't drive, and I was often stuck in the house alone in a whirlwind of thoughts and emotions. I wish I could say I had more support this time around, but my loneliness often got the best of me. I was scheduled for another C-section because my doctor thought laboring would be too hard on my body.

Shortly after I delivered another beautiful, perfect, healthy baby boy, I found myself again fending for myself and now two boys. My mom left to pursue her new career as a travel nurse. I didn't have many friends available or even willing to help. Their dad went to jail for 77 days shortly after I delivered him. I had to dig down deep for that strength again. Here I was, in the middle of a cold Wisconsin winter with a newborn and a five-year-old that needed to get to and from school every day.

Still healing from another major surgery, I had to bundle up my boys every morning at 7:30 am to get my oldest son to and from school. It's no wonder that my C-section incision ruptured and bled. I developed another infection. My doctor scolded me that I was supposed to be resting and not lifting anything heavier than the baby. I explained to her I didn't have a choice. I was doing it all alone. I had to do what I had to do because that is a requirement of being a mother.

I suffered more often from migraines. They would hit me like a semi-truck, but I didn't have time to be down. My doctor was convinced they were stress-induced headaches, but the thing was, I had no way to reduce any of the stress in my life. Another 5 years later, one of the worst migraines I ever had landed me back in the ER.

In 2012, I lost my job. To be honest, I was fired! I had never been fired before. I had no savings and was worried about how I would pay my bills. This completely overshadowed the fact that I was about to graduate from college with my Associate's degree in Fashion and Retail Marketing. I couldn't even be happy about my accomplishment I had worked so hard to achieve. The stress of losing my job while trying to finish school and taking care of two kids while their dad was in and out of jail, it was overwhelming. I didn't feel strong anymore. I relied so much on that inner strength, but it felt like it was failing me.

My migraines became more frequent and intense. I also suffered from low back and hip pain. Pregnancy and having anesthesia administered into your back can cause long lasting back pain. One day, this shooting pain went from my hip down my leg. I could barely walk because it was so painful. After an MRI scan and blood tests, the doctors couldn't determine the cause of the pain. They concluded that it was just inflammation. I was sent home with ibuprofen and was told to rest. That hip pain never went away. It still sneaks up on me often out of nowhere.

It was now 2013. I still hadn't found a job. I was living off unemployment checks and food stamps. Just like 10 years prior, I was still everything I never wanted to be. I was a single mom of two, jobless, broke, and living off of government assistance. Typical baby mama shit. Thankfully, President Obama extended the unemployment benefits and that got me through, so I could at least pay my rent.

One day in September, I had a pounding headache. It felt like what I imagined Tom would feel like when Jerry dropped an anvil on his head. The pain centralized on the left side of my head. My speech was slurred, my vision was blurry. I called my mom and tried to explain to her but I struggled to get the words out. It was like my brain and my body was disconnected. I was rushed to the ER because at 29 years old, they thought I was having a stroke.

In the ER, the nurses took me back immediately. I was hooked up to an IV, blood was drawn, and they did an MRI of my head. After what seemed like an eternity, the doctor finally came in and said, *"The good news is you didn't have a stroke. This is what we call a 'complex migraine,' and we think it was brought on by your pregnancy."*

What the hell did she just say?! I was stunned. They had to have the wrong test results, there was no way I was pregnant! I went into shock. I rocked back and forth and I even tried to pull the IV out of my arm. They probably thought I was crazy. The doctor was baffled, and said, *"You didn't know you were pregnant? I take it this is not good news."*

Um, no Doc, I did not know and, yes, it was absolutely the worst news I could've gotten! The ultrasound showed that I was already almost 10 weeks along. I had been on the birth control shot for a few years and then it dawned on me; I missed my shot the month before! I just couldn't believe that I got pregnant that fast. I found out on Monday I was pregnant and by Saturday their dad landed himself back in jail. At his court date, he was sentenced to 2 ½ years in prison.

I was so disappointed in myself. How did I let this happen yet again??!! No job, two kids and I was pregnant with baby number three. I sobbed for days. Maybe I should consider an abortion this time. I called around to different clinics for information and prices. I made the appointment. But, who was I kidding? I didn't even have the money to do it. Who in their right mind would bring another child into this situation? I pondered the decision for days. My mom warned me if I did it, I would regret it and I knew I would, so I went through with the pregnancy.

Pregnancy should be a happy and joyous experience. You are bringing new life into the world. It's unfortunate for me, that none of my pregnancies were that. Baby number three was no different. I went through yet another terrible nine months. I was just as sick as the first two times. I couldn't eat, even just the smell of food made me puke. I gained only 8 lbs. the whole pregnancy. I was so scared that my baby would be tiny and malnourished.

This baby was positioned towards my back and as he grew, he pressed onto my sciatic nerve so I was diagnosed with Sciatica. My back literally felt like it was on fire. I was even put into physical therapy because the back pain was so bad, and it eventually threw my back out of alignment. And, to top it all off, those damn migraines persisted throughout the entire pregnancy.

Depression sucked me into its abyss. I cried every day. It could've been my hormones out of whack, it could've been the disappointment in myself, it could've been the fact that I was doing it all alone, yet again, but it probably was a combination of all the circumstances, that made me a prisoner of my own thoughts. I was so nervous that my sadness would somehow transfer to my unborn baby. Would his temperament be sad? Would he cry all the time like I did? My doctor assured me he would be OK. You can't "transfer" depression to your baby. She prescribed me antidepressants, but I refused to take them. The risks to me and my baby outweighed the potential benefits, so I pushed through, like I had done so many times before.

We may not always realize it, but our bodies physically respond to stress. One day, I felt dizzy. I started shaking, my chest felt tight and my heart was beating 100 miles a minute. It felt like it would beat right out of my chest. I felt like I couldn't breathe. I was home with my two boys who were freaked out by the episode. I sat on the edge of my bed, trying to get myself together. I didn't know what was happening. The tightness in my chest felt like maybe I was having a heart attack. I hunched over in pain. My oldest son was smart enough to realize something wasn't right and called my mom. After about 10 minutes the episode subsided. My mom rushed over and said, *"I think you just had a panic attack."* I had a few more episodes like this during my third pregnancy.

According to adaa.org, (the Anxiety and Depression Association of America), *"A panic attack is the abrupt onset of intense fear or discomfort that reaches a peak within minutes."* Panic attacks are often accompanied by some of these symptoms; heart palpitations, pounding heart, or accelerated heart rate, sweating, trembling or shaking, shortness of breath feelings of choking, chest pain or discomfort, nausea or abdominal distress, feeling dizzy, unsteady or faint, chills or heat sensations, fear of losing control or "going crazy," and/or a fear of dying.

On top of having panic attacks, I started passing out again. My doctor urged that I had to reduce some of the stress in my life. She believed stress induced these symptoms of my pregnancy. Well, duh. But how was I supposed to do that?

5am the morning of my scheduled C-section, I called my mom hyperventilating. *"Mom, I can't do this. I don't want to have another baby! Why did I do this again? I am so stupid."* She quietly listened to me cry and assured me she was there to help me and that we would get through it. Deep down, I knew somehow it would be all right and that brought me some comfort, but that didn't stop me from sobbing the whole ride to the hospital.

I delivered another beautiful, healthy baby boy. Surprisingly, he was my biggest baby even though I gained only 8 lbs. He was a healthy 7 lbs. 12 oz. That little thief immediately stole my heart. My tears of melancholy quickly turned into tears of joy once I held him in my arms.

That joy was short-lived though as the overwhelming amount of responsibility I had slapped me silly. My sadness once again took over disguised as "baby blues," but it was so much deeper than that. "Baby blues" is common for many mothers after they have a baby. Moms can feel exhausted, worried, unhappy, or even feel trapped. We often cry over the smallest things. We may feel a decrease in our appetite and our sleep is all out of whack. It's also common to feel irritable or even nervous. The blues are caused by the physical and hormonal changes in our bodies. For some, it's hard to transition into motherhood or adjusting to having a new baby.

The curse of the C-section got me again as I

developed yet another infection in my incision. Once again me, doing too much too fast, had consequences. My body never got to properly heal because I was quickly propelled into the chaos that was my life, coupled with the demands of motherhood. I would suffer more panic attacks juggling taking care of three kids by myself, working full-time and trying to maintain my sanity.

Look. I blame no one for the direction my life took. I had this vision of being a young college-educated professional, in a big city, making money, going to swanky parties, and wearing designer dresses. Think, the biracial Carrie Bradshaw, curly locks and all. That's what I envisioned my life to be but that's not what it was. I was the girl that didn't even want kids and now I had 3! I made the choices and decisions that led to my life being how it was. I do, however, believe these series of events, illnesses, pregnancies, surgeries, coupled with stress definitely contributed to me eventually developing Fibromyalgia.

The effects of the things I went through still linger on now. Everything in life has a cause and effect. This was a period in my life where it felt like the bad always overshadowed the good and I just didn't know how much more I could take. Life seemed to beat me down and I just couldn't escape its grasp of negativity. My mom always said, *"God only gives the toughest battles to the strongest soldiers."* Damn, how strong did He think I was? Very strong, apparently, because life wasn't done with me yet.

5 DADDY LESSONS

My daddy was a gangsta. Point blank, period. He was about that life. I like to think I get a little bit of my edge from him. I'm quiet but I'm not a punk. He was cool, cocky, and confident. He was the smoothest talker you would ever meet. Maybe he got that swag from his own dad, because my granddaddy was a gangsta too. Gangsta is in my DNA and it's often how I approach things in life. I always have to be tough. I face things head on and as they come. I don't like to cry, but if I do I shed thug tears. And, my mom, well she wasn't a good girl either. She was rebellious and tough as nails. Once they linked up, my mom said they were like '84 Bonnie and Clyde.

My dad was African-American and my mom is Mexican-American which may have led to some identity issues for me, but that's a whole other story.

They grew up in the Gary, Indiana and met in high school. She got pregnant at 15 and had me when right after she turned 16. I was 4 weeks early and weighed only 4 lbs. She was just a baby having a baby.

Unfortunately, some of my earliest memories of my parents were them arguing and fighting. I witnessed the physical abuse of my mom as early as I can remember. I often see scenes in my head and I'll explain them to my mom. She is shocked by what I can remember. I can recall an instance where my dad was choking my mom. I remember screaming at him to, *"Stop hurting my mommy!"*

It's funny that I can remember those traumatic things, but "Fibro fog" now has me forgetting what day of the week it is. Go figure. I didn't understand that these were my memories, but I could see them so vividly. To think early trauma won't affect a child, even into adulthood, is a lie. These experiences are all directly related, and my therapist thinks so too.

Our little house on Pennsylvania street was sometimes calm and sometimes chaotic, but I don't remember feeling sad about it. Honestly, my mom did the best she could to make sure we were happy all while she masked her own sadness. She soon had my little brother and sister. She was 19 with three young kids. I remember my dad being in and out a lot but never really present or helping out.

One particular instance plays in my head like a movie. We were at my grandma's apartment. She lived upstairs and my aunt lived downstairs. We were upstairs and I remember hearing a commotion outside. I remember my dad yelling for my mom and the sound of the car horn blaring. I remember my brother and I excited to see him as we raced to the window to greet him, we waved and laughed and smiled. But, it wasn't a happy reunion.

He was hanging out of the car door, hollering for my mom to come out and waving something in his hand. My grandma and mom yanked us from the window and we got down low. Shots rang out. He was shooting at the house. I remember the sound but don't know if I knew what they were or what they meant. We stayed down low and snuck through the apartment, like army soldiers avoiding enemy fire, to the back door where we could go downstairs to the lower apartment. We were silent as chaos ensued outside. I don't know what his intentions were but eventually he left. My mom said later on that he was probably high on cocaine. We were in the middle of the crack epidemic that was the 80s. Crack cocaine ran rampant through black and brown neighborhoods, destroying communities and families.

I don't know how much time went past but after that incident my mom decided we had to leave town. She packed us up in a little orange 2 door hatchback that belonged to my aunt's boyfriend. We were piled in the back, my mom, my brother, sister, and I. She stuffed garbage bags of our belongings into the trunk and we left in the dark of the night. I didn't know where we were going, I don't know if my mom even knew, but we drove for miles. By the time we got to our destination, the sun was rising.

We ended up at this big house. As we approached the door, I gripped my Raggedy Ann doll tight, she brought me comfort. I was about five years old. These strangers fed and housed us. I now know it was a Battered Women's Shelter. My mom moved us to another state for our safety.

I would go back to Indiana often with my

grandma. I spent many summers there. I spent a lot of time at my great-grandparents' house too. I could always hear the shuffling in the kitchen and would look up from my sleep; it would still be dark out. They were up before the sun. My great-grandma Minnie would get up at the crack of dawn, literally, to make my great-grandpa his coffee and breakfast. *"Viejo!"* She would call him to the table. They would speak in Spanish and even though I didn't know what they were saying, it sounded like love to me. He would start the day reading his morning paper.

One morning my grandpa left his paper on the table. I sat down for breakfast and who do I see on the front page? My gangsta ass daddy. His mugshot plastered on the front page. He had robbed several stores and restaurants with a sawed-off shotgun. I was old enough to read and comprehend what I was reading. My grandma tried to grab the paper from my sight, but it was too late. I had seen what my dad was capable of. That incident was then tied to him stealing a car with a baby in it, which also led to a kidnapping charge. My dad was in and out of jail my whole life.

I don't remember seeing my dad again until

years later. I don't know how he got in contact with or found us. But, one day he showed up on our doorstep. My mom allowed him to have a relationship with us, but his priorities were always messed up. She never talked shit about him to us. She didn't paint him as a bad guy or make us hate him. I appreciate her for that. She let us form our own opinion and decide what our relationship with him would be and we didn't have to have one if we didn't want too.

One summer he took us to a carnival. My mom was reluctant about letting us go, but she did. We had so much fun with him. We rode the Ferris wheel and played games, he even won me a teddy bear. I slept with that bear every night. It was the only thing I had from my daddy. We got home and excitedly told our mom about the day we had with our dad. This might be the only happy memory I have with him and I still cherish it. He dropped us off and promised to come pick us up again the next weekend, but he never showed up. We waited and waited for him to come or call but he never did. Who knows what kept him from coming but for me, that was the point I decided I wanted nothing to do with him ever again and I stuck to that.

I discovered years later that he did 10 years in prison for attempted murder. He was paroled and by that time I was 18 and pregnant with my oldest son. He found us again and came in town. I remember him looking at me and telling me he was disappointed in me because I was pregnant. As if I wasn't already disappointed enough in myself, I didn't need his approval or blessing. The fact of the matter was that I was just as disappointed in him. I shrugged my shoulders and said, *"So,"* and that was the greeting of a father and daughter separated by so many years.

I gave him a dry ass side hug and went about my business. I had nothing to say to him and didn't care to hear anything he had to say. At that point, I was grown, and he couldn't tell me anything, even if he was my dad.

Isn't it funny how someone that wasn't present has so much presence in your life? The absence of my dad played, and still plays, so much of a role in my life even though I don't want it too. I never knew how much it affected me, and maybe a pivotal part in me developing these debilitating conditions. Physical and mental are very much connected.

My mental pain and anguish over not having my dad in my life affects me. He should have been there to teach me things, help me grow and guide me. But, that probably would have been like the blind leading the blind. My dad made lots of poor choices. I am actually the oldest of twelve kids. *"Papa was a rolling stone"*, for real. So, maybe in hindsight, it was better that he wasn't there to totally screw me up.

I can try to justify or rationalize it as much as I want, but it hurts that my dad wasn't in my life the way I needed him to be. He was my first experience with disappointment. I have abandonment and trust issues because of him. I longed for love I never got. I don't doubt that my dad loved me but I never heard him say it or show it. But, maybe he just didn't know how too.

I saw my dad here and there into adulthood. I took my boys to see him at his house once. We were standing in the yard talking and this stray pit bull came near us. His first reaction was to go grab a shotgun and shoot it in the air to scare the dog away. "Boom!" *Click, Click.* "Boom!" My kids were terrified and started crying. The intensity of the shotgun took me back to the apartment where years earlier he was shooting a gun trying to force us out of the house.

My dad and I talked on the phone sometimes, but we still never connected like a father and daughter should. Maybe it was my hurt that wouldn't let him get too close. I often ignored his calls or wouldn't call him back, and I regret that sometimes.

May 2, 2015 at 7am. I was awakened by numerous calls to my phone, back to back. I had missed calls and text messages from my uncle and sister. I finally answered, and my uncle said, *"Hi Catrina, this is your uncle Antwan. Sorry to wake you but I have some bad news. Your dad got shot last night and he died."* My heart dropped. I couldn't tell if I was in a dream or not. I didn't cry at that moment. I think I was still trying to process what he said. I was shocked, but then again, I wasn't. They say when you live your life in the streets you'll only end up one of two places, dead or in jail.

I, then, had to be the bearer of bad news. I called my brother, sister, and my mom to tell them. Once I talked to my mom, I completely broke down.

My feelings were all over the place. How could I be so sad about a man that was never there for me? I struggled with what I was supposed to feel. I cried and cried but I think I grieved the relationship we didn't get to have. I mourned his death but grieved his absence in my life. I was sad that we would never get another chance to try to have a relationship.

I was sad for my grandmother who lost her husband and son to homicide. I was sad for my other sisters and brothers, the youngest were about five and six. I secretly hoped that my dad would eventually turn his life around. But, at almost 50 years old, he still didn't have it figured out. His priorities still seemed to be the streets and not his kids or even his grandkids. I still had hope, even though nothing he ever said or did made me hopeful. After his death, I had the longest migraine I had ever experienced, one that overtook my entire body and lasted two weeks.

I cried the ugly cry at his funeral. My waterproof mascara was no match for the tears pouring from my eyes as it smeared across my face. At that moment, I wasn't a gangsta's daughter, I wasn't a mom, I was a little girl that needed her daddy and it hit me. He was dead. Regardless of the fact that he wasn't in my life, he didn't raise me, he was abusive, he did drugs, none of that mattered. That was still my dad and for that, I wept. On top of all that, I don't know if it was so much the fact that he died, but the way he did. *My dad was murdered.* Shot multiple times and left for dead in the parking lot of his "clubhouse". The place where he and his associates would meet and conduct gangsta business. Is it a coincidence he died there? Maybe. Is it even more coincidence he died as his own father did almost 30 years prior? Was it fate? Or Karma? Perhaps. The universe works in mysterious ways. But, we will never know.

At his funeral, I spoke on behalf of all his children, all 12 of us. I read an impersonal poem, one I found online about death, it was generic. But, it was the best I could do because I didn't have happy memories of him. He didn't teach me how to ride my bike, or swim, he didn't come to my recitals, he missed all of my birthdays, in fact I don't even think he knew when my birthday was. He missed everything in my life, so what was I supposed to say?

Before they closed his casket, I walked up to it with my own kids in hand to say our goodbyes. I bent over and whispered to him, *"Rest peacefully Dad. I forgive you."* I can't explain it but at that moment, I felt relief. I couldn't let that burden of hurt, anger, or resentment weigh me down any longer. I had to let it go. It took me years to be able to talk about it without crying. My only hope now is, that he is somehow guiding us in death how he never could in life.

6 A SERIES OF UNFORTUNATE EVENTS

L ife sure has a way of beating you down especially when you're already broken. As the saying goes, *"when it rains it pours,"* and Honey, I was in the middle of a hazardous hurricane with heavy winds and a torrential downpour.

Still trying to find healing after the sudden and tragic death of my father, I was trying to get back to normal. At this point, I was in a *very* stressful job as a supervisor in a call center. You have never known stress until you work in a customer service call center in an environment full of disgruntled employees acting like they are in high school, irate customers calling in to cuss you out over their missing packages, and whack ass upper management that sits on their asses doing absolute bare minimum all day. I hated my job. But, I had to do what I had to do, because you know, kids gotta eat.

My aunt Topeka was my dad's sister. I wish I had the chance to know her better or spend time with her. Sadly, she had a complete nervous breakdown and was diagnosed bipolar schizophrenic. My grandmother was taking care of her for 20 plus years. She was a college graduate, very smart, and beautiful. I feel like we were kindred spirits. My grandma Sara tells me how much I remind her of my aunt and how similar we were. The few times I visited my grandma, Topeka was always in her bedroom. She would peek out and say *"hi,"* then sneak back into her life of seclusion.

For months, she had this persistent cough that just wouldn't go away. My grandma begged her to go to the doctor and get it checked out, but she refused. She barely left the house. The cough got so bad she finally had to go see a doctor. An MRI of her lungs revealed that she had a tumor and it was cancer. The doctors couldn't pinpoint how long she had the cancer, but that it started in her breast and by the time she went in, it had already spread throughout her body. When they discovered it, she was already in stage 4 and her health was quickly declining.

My grandma put her in hospice care and within 3 months she had passed away. In one year, my grandma Sara lost two of her children. I lost a dad and an aunt. I can't imagine her pain, but I admired her strength. I like to think that I gained some of my own strength from her. A woman that survived a brain aneurysm, the murder of her husband, the murder of her son, and now the death of her only daughter. How can one woman survive so much? I developed a relationship with my grandma after my dad died and I appreciate her insight and wisdom. In every conversation we have, her words of caution are always the same. "*Slow down, baby. You have to take care of yourself and your health. You have to be around to take care of those babies. You are no good to anyone if you're not good to yourself.*" She may not realize it, but her words sit with me, in the pit of my stomach because I know she is right.

My migraines weren't letting up and the widespread pain in my body was increasingly present. I'm convinced I'm just overworking myself, I'm always on the go and I don't rest like I'm supposed too. I'm no different than any other working mom though. I have to suck it up and push through. There's too much to be done and I don't have time to be down. I don't complain about the pain, I take ibuprofen and I keep going. Even though the meds don't even seem to help, I take them anyway hoping to find some relief.

It's March 2016. I come home from another long day of being verbally degraded by customers, to my street being completely blocked off by police, fire trucks, and ambulances. The swirling of the red and blue lights illuminated the night sky. The Red Cross was on the scene as well as news cameras and reporters. I was so confused. What was going on? I just wanted to take a shower, get in my bed, and go to sleep! But I couldn't because a 5-alarm fire raged through my building.

The Red Cross was on sight to provide shelter and food for the night. Everything I owned was in that apartment! My boys and I stayed the night at my mom's house hoping to wake to some good news in the morning. Maybe it wasn't as bad as it seemed. Maybe they got it all under control and we could go back home. Nope. Not a chance. Life was playing this cruel joke on me, but I didn't find it funny.

It would be a week before the building was secure enough to assess the apartment and damages. By the time I got to walk through, my apartment was trashed. It smelled like mildew and was soaked with water. Black ash painted the white walls like the canvas of Picasso. I was heartbroken. My boys and I had just lost everything. A few things we could save but we were down to nothing. We had nothing. All that was left were memories of our 5 years at that address.

My family and a few friends stepped in to help us replace the material things we had lost. My feelings were hurt because the people I thought were close and would have my back, just didn't. My boys and I were homeless. I was trying to find us housing, buy new clothes for our backs, and food for our stomachs. My strength couldn't waver now. I had to stay strong, but slowly my body felt like it was breaking down. The pain in my limbs and joints seem to intensify as my headaches worsened. I couldn't let life beat me down though. I kept pushing and pushing. I had three little ones that depended on me. And, at the same time, another storm was quickly brewing ready to drown me.

My grandfather, "Papa", as we lovingly called him, was my father figure. He was the only man in my life that taught me things. He taught me how to swim, how to rollerblade, we traveled, we tried new food and restaurants. He always encouraged trying new things and experiences. I knew I could call him for any kind of advice. Papa was there for kindergarten graduation, middle school graduation, high school graduation, and college graduation. Papa was there for the important stuff. He was one of my biggest fans and supporters. In anything I did in life, he cheered me on. He was a master teacher of life.

We talked all the time, whether about politics or pop culture, didn't matter. We could talk about anything. And, Honey, he was an honorary member of the "Beyhive". He knew Beyoncé news before me and we would chat about her latest song, album, or music video. Our admiration for her was mutual. That still makes me giggle.

Papa was a no mess kind of guy. He was a

straight shooter and stone-faced. If something was wrong, he wouldn't let up. You wouldn't know because he didn't want you to know. But, I wish I would've known that he was ill. I now understand why he didn't want us to know. He wanted to keep things normal and he didn't want us to treat him like he was sick.

Papa had prostate cancer that eventually spread to his bones. He was silently suffering for a few years before a fall left him immobile. We didn't think it was that serious until he went into the hospital and never came out. This strong man I knew and looked up to was in the most fragile state I had ever seen him in. In the hospital was the first and only time I saw him cry. As if life hadn't thrown me enough blows already, Papa died. His absence is still felt in our family and it's been hard to go on without him.

My maternal grandma Phyllis, who I lovingly named "Brambi," is one of my best friends. Just like Papa, she is also one of my biggest supporters. I watched her, silently, from afar as she went through the illness with Papa. She tended to him, made sure he got the best treatment and took care of him. I watched her calmly plan and prepare for the worst. She didn't complain. Her strength never wavered and if it did, we didn't know it. She has been through a lot in life but she never lets you see her sweat. I admired how she smiled through her own sorrow and pain of losing her husband. I come from a long line of tough women so it's no wonder I always feel like I can take on the world. That strength is embedded in my bones.

I didn't know how much more I could take. My life was a shit show. What kind of karma was coming back around to me? What did I do to deserve all of the terrible things happening and so close together? Within less than two years, I had experienced 3 deaths in my family and lost everything in a fire. Me and life were in a 12-round bout. It felt like life would win by TKO. But I don't go down easy and not without a fight.

All the while, something was not right within me. My body was trying to tell me something, but I didn't have the time to listen. My spirit was sad, but I walked around every day with a faded smile, pretending to be OK. But inside, I was ripping apart at the seams. I was convinced someone was doing voodoo over my life.

7 I AM THE EXPERT OF ME

If I know nothing else in life, I know myself. And I knew that something was not right. These persistent pains in my body, they just wouldn't let up. I had neglected myself for such a long time that my body was screaming out for help. If my body could talk, she probably would've snapped on me and said, *"Look Bitch, you better get your shit together and get checked out before I completely shut the fuck down on your dumb ass."*

My body's inner voice is ratchet as fuck. It's all the ratchet I have to keep buried down deep inside because I grew up in the hood but went to school in the suburbs and I've always worked in corporate white spaces where Becky calls me "Tina" instead of "Trina" and I speak with a fake ass customer service voice. Don't act brand new, you know the one, because you use it too!

I was experiencing more consistent pain throughout my body. After months of ongoing pain, mood changes, and headaches, it was finally time to see a doctor. As simple as that may seem, it wasn't easy to get a diagnosis.

I saw a primary care doctor, Dr. P. Our first visits were fine. She was nice enough and seemed to listen to my concerns. She was convinced that my pain was nothing more than me overworking myself. To be sure she sent me to see an Orthopaedic doctor, which is a doctor that specializes in issues pertaining to the musculoskeletal system. That was a colossal waste of time. The exam was literally him tapping on some of my joints, examining my back and hips and asking me a few questions. He concluded, in a thick Indian accent, and I quote, *"There's nothing physically wrong with you. You are probably just overworking yourself. It's the repetitive motions you do every day. Try taking ibuprofen for pain."* And he walked out. That was it. I felt so dismissed and I was treated like my pain was just a figment of my imagination. And, maybe it was. I started to doubt myself.

I went back to see Dr. P and told her I didn't

agree with the Ortho doctor and ibuprofen for pain wasn't cutting it. I felt like Dr. P wasn't getting it either. This was much more than me overworking myself and I didn't feel like my doctor was trying to get to the root of the problem. She eventually sent me to physical therapy.

My physical therapist, Kelly, was my turning point. After a few months together, she and I were building a great rapport. I felt like she listened and addressed my pain. We tried different movements and exercises, but I think we both knew it wasn't really working. One day, Kelly said, *"There's something else going on with you. I'm trying to figure it out, but I want you to get another opinion on your pain."* And she referred me to Dr. M.

Before I went to see Dr. M, I was talking to my mom about everything I had encountered with the different doctors and how I felt like I was getting nowhere. I was frustrated because the pain was getting worse and I wasn't getting any relief. My mom told me that unfortunately, she saw this all of the time working in the medical field. She said many times when you are young, appear healthy, and tests come back negative, doctors will often dismiss you. They will give you the simplest explanations and not dig deep to figure out what is really going on, and that is very problematic.

My mom unofficially diagnosed me. She said, *"Have you ever heard of Fibromyalgia? I think you need to bring it up to your doctor and see what they say. I have a sneaking suspicion that is what you have. I really hope not because it is painful, and you will have it for the rest of your life. And it gets worse the older you get."* Yikes!

I had never heard of this condition before. I immediately went to Google. As soon as the description came up it was like a lightbulb went off over my head. I had almost all the symptoms and the synopsis of the illness fit me to a tee. While it was relieving to maybe have an answer, I was also saddened to think I have something that's not curable and I will likely endure pain for the rest of my life. While it would be nice to have a diagnosis, I really didn't want this one.

At my appointment with Dr. M, I explained to his nurse my symptoms and how nothing was helping or working. She immediately said, *"Sounds to me like you suffer from Fibromyalgia.*" I didn't even have to bring it up, based on my symptoms, the nurse knew, just like my mom did. And Dr. M agreed. But before he gave me a confirmation, he had me go for lab work and some MRI scans to rule out other inflammatory conditions like arthritis or rheumatoid arthritis. The Fibromyalgia "test" consists of checking 18 trigger points on the body to see if you react to them. If the doctor presses the point and it's painful, tender and you have a painful reaction to 11 out of 18 of them, you are diagnosed with Fibro. I reacted to 12. We also discovered that I suffer from carpal tunnel syndrome in my hands and fingers.

It was time to figure out a treatment plan. There are a few medications on the market approved to treat Fibromyalgia. It has been trial and error with different dosages, frequency, and which ones to take. I didn't do well with the side effects and none worked for me. I appreciate Dr. M because he took the time to hear me out, he addressed my concerns and he didn't dismiss me because I was young or because I "looked healthy".

All good things don't last forever. I had a

great relationship with Dr. M. I felt like he understood me and my needs as a patient. I was happy with his care, that was until the medical bills started to pile up. Because of how the insurance through my employer worked, it cost me every time I would see Dr. M. And, initially, that's was a lot. I had multiple visits as we addressed my Fibro, migraines, and he officially diagnosed me with depression. Due to cost and insurance, I had to switch providers. I dreaded it because I really liked Dr. M.

I started seeing Dr. H. Our first visit went great but that was short lived. Every visit with Dr. H seemed to be more of the same. She made the same suggestions every time. *"Try yoga, try water aerobics, try walking every day, try Tai Chi."* She was beginning to sound like a broken record, but let me explain. In people with Fibromyalgia, low, moderate exercise can help reduce pain. But, in some people it can make the pain and flare-ups worse. I am one of those people. I will do some light exercise, and feel really great. But usually the next day, I feel like I got hit by a bus.

I tried Dr. H's suggestions. Every time I try to exercise, I pay for it. For me, it feels counterproductive because everything in my body throbs. I explained this to Dr. H but it's like she didn't get it. I was over Dr. H after only a few months of seeing her. It felt like she addressed me like I was a child instead of a 30- something mother of 3, like she knew what was best for me. It felt like she was talking at me and not to me. I once left her office in tears because we literally disagreed on what my treatment plan should be. I expressed to her I needed some time off. I needed a mental break. I needed some time to stop, breathe, and just have the time to take care of myself. She responded that she wouldn't grant me any time off because she believed I would lie around in the bed all day.

In my head I was like, *"Bitch, what?"* I am the mother of 3, how in the hell would I be able to lie around in the bed all day? I have shit to do, all day, every day, but rarely does that time allow time to take care of myself. I guess she wasn't convinced that a mental health break was necessary. She wasn't being helpful, she felt like her plan was the best and only plan and I should just stick to it. Except, her plan wasn't working.

A doctor-patient relationship should be collaborative. We should work together to figure out the best treatment plan and explore different options. If that's not what I'm getting from my doctor, I will find a different one with the quickness.

This is where I learned that I had to be an advocate for myself and my health. I had to do my research and be empowered with information. Doctors don't know everything. One doctor's diagnosis or treatment is not the end all, be all. This is where it helps to talk to others with the same condition and find referrals.

I think, sometimes, people get stuck and feel like they have to stick with one doctor and what that doctor says, goes. That's false. It's always a good idea to get a second or even third opinion.

I learned that I had to take control of my care. I will not be demeaned or dismissed or treated like my pain isn't real because it is. I am the expert of me. Nobody, not even a doctor, truly knows what's best for me and my healing. We should be able to work together to figure that out. Being an advocate for yourself means taking responsibility for your wellness and wellbeing. It also means taking the time and energy needed for your own self-care. Remember what I said before? *"Self-care is important and necessary."*

Eventually, I went back to Dr. M, despite the medical bills. He made me the most comfortable and would hear me out. At my return visit, he and his assistant welcomed me back with open arms. We talked through everything I had tried, what the other doctor's plans were and we started a new treatment plan and I actually felt some relief.

In this journey, I also figured out that I had to educate myself on my conditions so when I went to doctor visits I was armed with information and questions. When informed, it's easier to work with your doctor to figure out the best approach to your care. Besides the internet, it was helpful for me to connect with other people suffering from the same conditions. I joined support groups online and also took the time to talk to other Fibromyalgia sufferers. It's more common than I thought, so it wasn't hard to find people to talk to about it. Those people had a wealth of knowledge from their own experiences.

8 DON'T SUFFER IN SILENCE

I dabble in acting a little bit, here and there. I've been in some short films and plays in the local community theater. It's something I've always liked to do. I killed it as "Cha Cha," in my middle school's rendition of *"Grease."*

I was in a play called, *"The Butterfly Confessions,"* by Yetta Young. It was a beautiful experience working with a range of different women, sharing our own personal stories in the process of putting on the play. It was a wonderful display of sisterhood and support. The play itself explored the many facets and experiences in the lives of women of color. The piece I performed was called, *"Sistas Don't Do Therapy."* In a nutshell, the piece suggests that black women don't go to therapy because we are taught to be strong, handle things as they come, and we don't "put our business out in the streets." We are taught, whether intentionally or not, to suffer in silence.

According to the National Alliance on Mental Illness, *"While Black Americans are 20% more likely than the general population to develop mental health problems (and Black women are more likely to experience and mention physical symptoms related to mental health problems), only a quarter of Black Americans seek care, compared to 40% of white people."*

Therapy is "taboo" in our community. We're not supposed to expose ourselves on such a deep and intimate level. We are supposed to stay strong and not fold. We are supposed to keep our feelings at bay, bottled up inside. But the thing about that is, eventually those feelings will erupt, and you will explode. Maybe you've tried to reach out to your sister, mother, or aunt to only be told, *"You'll be OK, just pray on it."* But, "prayer without work," doesn't work! Sometimes, you have to take the bull by the horns and face your problems head-on. The thing is, if you don't get to the root cause of your issues, you will forever be chained to them.

Often, I just felt stuck. Like I was in this rut or funk I just couldn't pull myself out of. I felt like I was sinking in an ocean of despair with no life jacket, just trying to keep my head above water. Sometimes you just get to the point that your spirit is tired. No matter how happy you try to be, you're just not. And that's OK, but you have to figure out a way to cope. You can't live in that space for too long. That's where therapy can be a great resource.

I am an advocate for therapy. I believe it is helpful to talk to someone with a 3rd party objective view. To be in an unbiased, non-judgmental environment where you are free to speak your mind and voice your feelings. Therapy is a form of self-care and I wish more people would utilize it. There is such a stigma about mental health and getting help, particularly in communities of color, and we need to break away from that.

According to the Substance Abuse and Mental Health Services Administration, *"One in five American adults suffer from some form of mental illness and only about 46-65 percent with moderate-to-severe impairment are in treatment."* Why is that? Maybe it's the lack of diversity in the mental health field that can be discouraging. Maybe we think only "crazy" people go to therapy or that if we seek help, it's a sign of weakness, but it is not.

We all need to deal with our shit and let's be honest, we all have shit. Whether it's childhood trauma, physical abuse, emotional abuse, stress, whatever, it's our responsibility to unpack that baggage. We owe it to ourselves to live our best lives because we only get this one. True enough, we can't always control situations that happen but what we are in control of is how we respond to them. That also means not living in a negative space of hurt, anger and resentment for the shit that has happened to us. Sometimes, it means forgiving those who have wronged us. It doesn't mean you have to forget, but forgiveness is more for you than that person. *See, I learned that in therapy.*

When we learn to forgive and let go, it almost releases that burden we carry around with us. It takes energy to be angry. It takes energy to be hurt. Why would you want to waste your precious energy holding onto all that crap? That shitload can get very heavy and weigh you down. And sooner or later, that shit starts to smell.

I am a big believer in Energy. The type of energy you put out into the world, is often what comes back to you. It is so easy to get sucked into a negative space, especially when you don't feel good every day. While it's easier said than done, staying as positive as you can will help you to cope and feel better. If everything you do or say is negative or you harbor negative energy, you will never fully heal, whether physically or emotionally.

I started seeing a therapist after my dad was killed. It was such a traumatic event that unleashed so many feelings in me. Not just the grief or the sense of loss, but unpacking the events in my childhood. My dad's absence was a void in my life. I knew I could no longer deal with these issues on my own. I had to talk to somebody to begin the process of healing.

I immediately felt like I could open up and talk to my therapist. She offered me the gift of perspective. She made me see people, situations, and the stuff I was dealing with from different points of view. Sometimes, our view can get obstructed especially when we see things in a negative light. Trying to process things through a lens of hurt or anger will always leave our vision blurred.

I was constantly pouring from an empty cup. By giving and giving of myself, my time, my energy, my cup didn't stay full. Then, through therapy, I realized that sometimes I have to refill my own cup, and those refills are free. Sometimes, the things we feel like we aren't getting in life, we have to give ourselves. Whether it is praise, love, safety, or even security. We can't always depend on the people in our lives to fulfill those needs. Sometimes, we have to love ourselves enough to make sure our cup runneth over. And from that run over, we can give.

I had to realize my own self-worth and had to stop seeking external validation. I am important as well as my needs. My self-perception and self-worth is owned entirely by me and not the world. I figured out my worth, and in that, I am worthy of being loved and appreciated. If someone isn't giving me what I need then I don't need them in my life. Simple. I am also responsible for the hurt I allow in my life. I couldn't control that as a child, but I can control it now. I had to realize that *people only treat me how I allow them to treat me.* True, I can't control anybody's actions, but I can control letting them be in my life. That awareness alone is empowering.

It will take time to build a relationship and trust with a therapist. For me, being a woman of color, it was important that my therapist was also a woman of color. Our struggles, our life experiences, our strengths are just different, but it's also a part of the things we, as women of color, have in common. I thought another black woman would understand me a little bit better. Maybe even relate. And I felt that with my therapist. She doesn't judge me, but she holds me accountable. She is open and honest and I know with her, I am still in control of my treatment because we work together.

Therapy helps you work through your stuff but the other great thing is it gives you the tools to cope. Having those tools will also help you deal with future problems. Because mental and physical are deeply connected, working through the mental might help ease up some of the physical ailments.

Do you find yourself "self-medicating?" Maybe drinking or smoking your worries away? Therapy helps you work through the things that might cause you to self-medicate. Self-medicating doesn't heal anything, it tricks your mind into thinking you are feeling better, but only for a short amount of time. I found myself having a glass of wine, maybe two, almost every day after work. I knew it couldn't be healthy and could only lead to a long-term problem, especially since drug and alcohol addiction runs in my family.

While promoting my own healing, I've found myself being better able to cope with life. But, with the tools I've learned, I can foster a healthy environment for my children. My kids know it is OK to talk about their feelings. Even in our hyper-masculine society, I let my boys know that it is OK to cry and I don't make them feel bad or weak for doing so. I want my boys to know that they can come and talk to me about anything and they won't be judged. Their feelings are valid and important and will not be minimized.

Think of yourself like an onion. You are made up of many layers and the only way to get to each layer is to peel them back. You have to be willing and able to expose each layer, no matter how stinky it may be. That's what therapy can help you do. Peel back those emotional layers so you can begin healing. Expose your truths and deal with it!

9 UNBREAK MY HEART

I used to love that song. It's a classic love ballad. Can't you just remember Toni Braxton in that silver, side cut out dress on the stage belting out in her deep alto, *"Unbreak my heart, say you love me again?"* I don't know if that's possible, for someone to unbreak your heart but what if it is up to us to unbreak our own heart? Unbreak our heart from pain, trauma, drama, and stress so we can properly heal.

Maybe some of my physical pain is being caused by the pain in my heart. I've been hurt by so many people that said they loved me, but they only ended up hurting me. People like my dad, my first love, my children's father, friends that turned into foes and even family. We've all heard that "love hurts", but that is a lie. Love isn't supposed to hurt, and it doesn't. Love is happy, love is joy, love is your children, love is a sunny day. The statement that love hurts is a facade, because the love does not hurt, it's the pain caused by the one you love, that actually hurts us. We then associate that pain with love. We hold onto that pain so tight that it can consume us. We dwell in that hurt when we need to learn how to let it go.

And to be honest, I'm still working on that in my own journey. My children's father and I have been through a lot together but we are in a better place now. We are trying to learn how to better communicate how we feel and forgiving each other for past hurt. And I admire the father he is to our boys and his own growth. Growth, whether in ourselves or others, takes time so we have to be patient.

We also have to understand that you can't always expect the person who hurt you to heal you. You have to love yourself enough to heal yourself. Listen, I am no expert in love but I am an expert in *loving myself*. Self-love is probably the most important relationship I will ever have. It's the relationship I have with myself and the one I will have forever. It includes nobody else, it is not dependent on anyone else, it can't be fulfilled by anyone else. I am solely responsible for how I love and treat myself which ultimately leads to my happiness. When we learn how to love ourselves enough, we open up our heart to not only give love, but receive it too.

And that can be hard for some people. Healing from past hurt can take a long time, but if you are working at it, you can get through it. I was very guarded for a long time. I didn't let people in easily and I was always suspicious of their intentions. Maybe it's the Scorpio in me, but it could also be the hurt I carry disguising itself as a shield of armor to protect my heart. Many times, when I let people close, I get fucked over in the end. *"When people show you their true colors, believe them,"* Maya Angelou once said. I am the protector of me and my energy, so I am cautious of whom I let into my circle.

I came to the realization a long time ago that I always had to have my own back. When I think I can depend on people, I usually can't. The people I expected to be there for me just weren't. I had to accept that I couldn't expect people to treat me or be there for me like I would be for them. It's a hard pill to swallow, but it's the truth. It's good I figured that out before I was diagnosed with any conditions, because people rarely check on the strong friend. *Check on your strong friend!* Like Beyoncé said, *"Me, myself and I, that's all I got in the end."* I am strong because I have to be. That was until I realized I actually have a strong support system.

Loving yourself is also being aware of who is around you and the energy they harbor. Other people's energy can affect you. Have you ever been around a co-worker in a bad mood? It just puts a damper on the day.

My circle is full of my "sista-friends" who speak life into me, who motivate me, who call me out on my BS. The ones who, occasionally promote a little ratchetness, but keep it real. They are the ones that "check on the strong friend," because ultimately, we check in on each other. We laugh, we talk, we encourage each other, offer each other advice and journey on this thing called life together.

The members of your tribe should have your

best interests at heart, as you have theirs. You are there for each other. There's no drama, no backstabbing, no jealousy or envy but instead light, love, and laughter when you're around each other. It's so important to have a strong support system. It should be made up of people who actually show up when they say they will, allow us to expose all parts of ourselves and be people who provide us with what we need and how we need it.

Attempting to practice self-love, self-care and self-compassion can be even more difficult when you suffer from depression. There is already this skewed view on yourself and your life that it can be hard to invoke the positive feelings. The poet Rumi wrote, *"Your task is not to seek for Love, but merely to seek and find all the barriers within yourself that you have built against it."* Depression can feel like a barrier to loving yourself fully. But, at some point, we have to accept who and what we are and what we've been through.

When we let love into our lives whether it's love of self or love from others, it feels good. Self-love is the appreciation we have for ourselves and doing things that foster healthy physical, emotional and even spiritual growth. It's being compassionate with yourself and how you are feeling. Sometimes, we get so wrapped up in what is happening to us or what has happened to us, we forget to express love for ourselves. We must learn how to indulge ourselves in self-love and self-care. But, in learning how to do that, we have to practice patience with ourselves as we learn how to do so.

Research has shown that greater self-love and self-compassion leads to less anxiety and depression, more optimism and even better recovery from stress. Having compassion for yourself means treating yourself with the same love, kindness, care, and concern you would show your friend or even family member.

Practicing good self-care is so important because it leads to greater self-love. We have to learn how to take care of our own basic needs. We can do that by making healthy choices for ourselves. This can be anything from making better food choices, getting some daily exercise, being involved in healthy relationships and activities, doing some yoga or even mediation. Self-care is limitless and is up to you.

There is no specific plan for self-care, but, at the end of the day, it's *you taking care of you.*

I learned as I practiced better self-care routines that I had to set boundaries for myself and people in my life. My brother stays involved in many unhealthy things, and because he's my brother I always want to help him out. I always tried to be there for him, however I could, but what I realized is being there for him was draining me. I had to step out of the situation to realize I can't help someone that doesn't want to help themselves.

I continued to let him break my heart, because as his sister, I care deeply for him and his well-being. But, I can't care more about him than he cares for himself. I also can't care about him more than I care for myself, no matter how guilty it made me feel. He continued to make poor choices, landing himself in trouble and getting involved with drugs and alcohol, but those were his choices alone and he has to deal with the consequences.

I had to realize that whatever my brother had going on, had nothing to do with me. By setting boundaries with him and refusing to participate in his problems, I stop inflicting that stress on myself. You realize that with love, y*ou can love someone but love them from a distance.* I learned that it is OK to be selfish when it comes to my own happiness and sanity, even if that means keeping my time, energy and love to myself, for myself.

My journey of self-love also means living intentionally. I intend to live a good, fulfilled, loving, happy life. The only way to achieve this is to do things and make decisions that promote my overall wellbeing and promotes growth. Keeping myself feeling loved, for me, means setting out realistic goals and while accomplishing them, giving myself praise. Sometimes, we forget to give our own selves a pat on the back for a job well done. I am hard on myself, but I am learning to take it easy and even if I fail at something, there is still something to be learned. Accepting the fact that I am human and I will make mistakes, helps me to love myself more.

I love affirmations. It's the small things we say to ourselves when we start our day or even at the end of one. When we continually speak life into ourselves eventually we truly start to believe it. They say when you do something 21 days in a row, it becomes a habit. Affirming yourself can be a positive and healthy habit to get into. Saying something like, *"I am worthy of love,"* or *"I am enough,"* or what about, *"I am exactly who I need to be."* What is your self-talk like? How do you speak to yourself or about yourself?

One of my favorite writings is, *"As I Began to Love Myself,"* by Charlie Chaplin. Reading it helps me to reflect on what it means to have love for myself.

I love this passage," *As I began to love myself I freed myself of anything that is no good for my health, food, people, things, situations, and everything that drew me down and away from myself. At first, I called this attitude a healthy egoism. Today I know it is the love of oneself."*

Unbreaking my own heart helps me with my emotional healing, which I believe helps me with my physical healing. In my journey, I've had to learn how to slow down, set boundaries, and live intentionally. By doing so, I've developed a greater amount of love and respect for myself. Realizing my own worth is powerful, yet empowering. It's not selfish nor is it egotistical to have a healthy, loving, positive relationship with yourself.

10 **FIX MY FIBRO**

(Please note: I am not a medical professional. These are just my suggestions. Please speak with your doctor before you try anything new.)

A s you can see, living with invisible illnesses is a complex thing. We don't always understand why we develop these conditions, but the key is how we deal with them. Fibromyalgia, in particular, is tricky. There is no cure for it and it's a baffling disease, even to the medical community. What causes it? Is it our pain receptors, our nerves, perhaps our imagination?! **eye roll** Who knows? There are multiple theories, but still no concrete answers.

If you have suffered from ongoing widespread pain for over three months, have terrible fatigue, headaches, and/or cognitive issues, it may be time to talk to your doctor. If you think you may suffer or maybe are newly diagnosed with Fibromyalgia, here's some of the advice I wish I had in the beginning and some of my own tips and tricks.

There are drugs approved to treat the symptoms of Fibro, but none cure it. In fact, it is noted that medication works for only about 30%-50% of Fibromyalgia patients. I tried the approved drugs, and for me, the side effects were worse than the symptoms. I felt like a groggy zombie, sleepily making my way through each day. It was awful. However, for some people, the medications work. And that's awesome for them! The medications may work better with a treatment plan of other lifestyle changes. It's a series of trial and error to figure out what may work for you, so you must be patient. It can take months before you notice any difference.

Some topical analgesics help to numb the pain. Although they don't completely take the pain away, they can help take the edge off. Again, it will be trial and error with what may work for you, but I personally like to use Tiger Balm. Yes, the smell is strong as hell, but I can find some pain relief when I rub it onto my joints. Another thing to try is to take a bath in Epsom Salt. Epsom Salt is thought to ease stress, relax the body, relieve pain, and helps muscles and nerves function properly. A long, hot bath is relaxing anyway, just add a little Epsom Salt to it to help combat some of the pain.

Try keeping a journal of your symptoms. Every day rate your pain level on a scale of 1-10. Record what hurts and describe what the pain is like (throbbing, shooting). Are there any particular triggers? Do you feel more pain if the weather changes? Do you experience more pain when it's extremely hot or extremely cold? What about your diet? Do you feel better or worse if you eat or drink particular things? By keeping a written record, you can notice patterns of pain, which may lead to you avoiding certain triggers.

It is believed that certain foods and drinks can trigger pain. Listen, I was a Pepsi addict! I drank soda all day every day but I found once I reduced my caffeine intake, I noticed a decrease in my pain. I also increased my water intake, which was so hard for me, but I believe it has helped with my overall wellness. There are so many benefits to drinking water that can help with managing pain. Being dehydrated can affect your mood, memory, and your sensitivity to pain and can cause headaches. We flush out toxins in our body when we regularly consume water.

I heard this once and it was easy to remember. Stay away from **C.R.A.P**.! By limiting **C**arbonated drinks, **R**efined sugars, **A**rtificial sweeteners, and **P**rocessed foods, I noticed an overall better feeling in my mood and pain. I incorporated more fruits and vegetables into my diet and I try to stay away from sweets, (which is so hard because I have such a sweet tooth!) Research suggests trying a plant-based, vegetarian, or even vegan diet might help.

One thing I wasn't doing before was taking vitamins. I incorporated a daily multivitamin along with Vitamin D and Vitamin B12. My doctor tested me for a Vitamin D deficiency, which I had. It's not uncommon for people without much exposure to the sun to have the deficiency. Vitamin D can help combat chronic pain. People with B vitamin deficiencies may experience depression, anxiety, mood swings, and fatigue. Vitamin B12, in particular, is thought to help increase your energy. Fibromyalgia can cause sleeplessness that causes fatigue which weighs heavily on your energy levels. This vitamin also benefits your nervous system and some medical professionals believe Fibro is caused by overactive nerves.

Dr. M told me initially that for some people, exercise helps the condition, and for others it makes the Fibro pain worse. For me, too much activity heightens my pain. However, I don't want to be a couch potato either, so I try to do low impact, light movements to keep my body moving. Even just taking a walk on my break or light yoga stretches helps me to combat pain. The fact is a lack of exercise leads to greater muscle weakness and more fatigue, so try to move when you can. The key is to start at a low and steady pace and be as consistent as you can.

As you deal with your physical pain, don't forget to address your emotional well-being. Getting a diagnosis like this is life changing. Deal with those feelings. Take time to deal with and reflect what is happening to you. Try joining support groups and talk to other people dealing with the same conditions. One thing that helps me is journaling. I like to sit with myself and just write. There's no rhyme or reason to journaling, just write what you feel. It can be very therapeutic.

Meditate. Meditation has been around for centuries and is thought to have positive effects and benefits. To be in a meditative state is to be a true state of awareness. It is believed that meditation has short-term benefits on the nervous system and helps to feel less anxiety, less stress, and experience deeper relaxation. Although a simple practice, daily meditation can have long-lasting effects which can reduce stress, increase calmness, clarity, and promote happiness. Mindful meditation can help promote a good night's sleep.

Sleep. Especially when in pain, getting proper rest is imperative, but it also is hard to get because the pain can interrupt your sleep. Being sleep deprived causes fatigue which then triggers cognitive problems like Fibro fog. You have to practice healthy sleeping habits and maybe get into a bedtime ritual. Try to avoid screen time an hour before bed, no TV, no phone, no tablet. Maybe take a hot bath and avoid drinking too much caffeine during the day. If you must, don't drink it after 4pm. There are small changes we must make to be well and feel better. Proper rest is important when dealing with any illness.

I like to use essential oils in a diffuser in my room and make myself a cup of "sleepy time" tea at night. The biggest lie I believed as a child is that naps were a punishment! Honey, I live for a good nap now and I don't feel guilty about taking one either! Nap when you need too. If I am having trouble falling asleep, I also like to listen to sleep meditations on YouTube.

Say NO. I have a really hard time with this and I am notorious for overextending myself and I always pay for it! I still try to be social and hang out with my friends, but I realized that I can't make every function, whether for friends or family. Sometimes, we need that time for ourselves to recoup and recover and hopefully people will understand that. I feel bad when I have to miss one of my son's football or basketball games, but I try not to miss too many. The reality is I can't be a good mom to them if I'm not taking care of myself. I believe my boys understand that now.

Pace yourself. When I am having a good day, I will try to do so much and accomplish lots of things. I had to learn that I have to pace myself and ask for help when I need it. The dishes won't always be done, and the laundry is never-ending so don't force yourself. It is what it is! You can only do so much. I was so determined to get my half-bathroom painted. I call it the "Babe Cave." It's the only place I have in my house to get ready. I took two weeks to paint it because I had to keep stopping and taking breaks. Something that can seem easy for most, is hard to do when you live with pain.

My biggest piece of advice would be to be open to other healing treatments and therapies. Yes, there is traditional Western Medicine, but what about Eastern Medicine remedies? What about massage therapy, talk therapy, Reiki, acupuncture, or aromatherapy? Your treatment and healing is entirely up to you. Do your research, be empowered and educated about all options available. Work with your doctor to incorporate other healing methods into your treatment plan. If your doctor isn't open, ditch him and find a doctor who is.

I hope for your healing, not only physical but mental and emotional. I hope my story has enlightened you, inspired you, or maybe even educated you, but overall I hope my words, in some way, have helped you. I wish you love and light on your own journey. ♥

ABOUT THE AUTHOR

T rina is a writer at heart, but is also a speaker and performer. Her love for words and writing began at an early age. She was the editor of her middle school newspaper, high school newsletter and contributed articles to her college newspaper as well, so it's no surprise that she has finally penned her first book. She has performed and published original poetry and spoken word pieces. Her true love is creative & fiction writing.

"Fly Girl with Fibro", is her first published book and she has a blog by the same name. Her hope is to bring awareness to the condition and educate, encourage and empower others living with any kind of invisible illness.

She is the mother of three beautiful boys, Jamier, Isaiah and Elijah who are her ultimate motivation.

Made in the USA
Monee, IL
24 April 2023